KID GUARDIANS®
JUST BE SAFE ™
SERIES

I Know Where I Live

by
Diane H. Pappas
& Richard D. Covey

Illustrated by
Ric Estrada

SCHOLASTIC INC.
New York Toronto London Auckland Sydney
Mexico City New Delhi Hong Kong Buenos Aires

To my son Nikos with love — you inspire me every day.
— D.H.P.

To my wife, Loretta, and our children, Aaron, Marc, Aleli,
Rebekah, Seth, Jeremy, Ethan, Hannah, and of course Zilia,
and their spouses and children with love
— R. E.

Thanks to the artists of The Pixel Factory (special thanks to Bob & Desma)
for contributing their talents to the creative production of these books.

———————————————

ISBN 0-439-88032-7

Printed in the U.S.A.
First printing, September 2006

MEET THE KID GUARDIANS®

From their home base in the mystical Himalayan mountain kingdom of Shambala, Zak the Yak and the Kid Guardians® are always on alert, ready to protect the children of the world from danger.

ZAK THE YAK is a gentle giant with a heart of gold. He's the leader of the Kid Guardians®.

Loyal and lovable, **SCRUBBER** is Zak's best friend and sidekick.

BUZZER is both street-smart and book-smart and not afraid to show off.

Always curious about the world, **SMOOCH** loves to meet new people and see new places.

CARROT is full of energy and the first to jump in when help is needed.

Whenever a child is in danger, the **TROUBLE BUBBLE**™ sounds an alarm and then instantly transports the Kid Guardians® to that location.

"Hurry, Dad! We are almost at the pandas!" called Neal.

"I can't wait to see the new cubs!" added Susie.

"Just a minute, kids," said Susie's mother. "I want to give the baby her juice."

"Where did Susie and Neal go?" asked Susie's father. "They
were here just a minute ago."

"They must have wandered off to find the panda cubs while we
were busy with the baby," said Susie's mother.

"Which way are the panda cubs?" asked Susie. "Neal, where are we?"
"I don't know. I think we're lost," said Neal nervously.

"Look, Zak!" Smooch shouted. "Those kids need our help. Let's go!"

Zak and Smooch arrived in a flash and introduced themselves to Neal and Susie.

"Hi, kids! Don't worry. I'm Smooch and this is Zak the Yak. Our job is to keep kids safe. We're going to help you find your parents."

"Can you tell me your name?" Zak asked Susie.

"My name is Susie," she replied shyly.

"What is your last name?" Zak asked.

"I can't remember," Susie answered.

"Susie," said Zak, "it's very important for you to know your full name." "You should also learn your address and telephone numbers," added Smooch. "This will help us find your parents."

"My name is Neal Alexander, and my address is 3050 Maple Street, San Diego, California," announced Neal proudly. "Oh, and I know my mom's cell phone number."

"Very good, Neal!" said Henry. "I'm going to call your mom right now and tell her that you're both safe."

"Neal and Susie are at the Lost and Found office!" exclaimed Neal's mother. "Neal gave them my cell phone number."

Susie's and Neal's parents hurried to the Lost and Found office. They were so relieved to see their kids!

"Oh, Neal, I'm so glad you knew your mom's cell phone number," Susie's mom said. "Now we know how important it is for Susie to learn mine."

"I know you two will never run off alone again," said Zak. "But if you ever get separated from your parents, it's important to know your full name, your address, and your telephone numbers."

"I don't ever want to get lost again," said Susie.

"Just remember what you learned today and you won't have to worry," Smooch told her.

Let's remember what we have learned.

Be sure you know:

- Your full name
- Your complete address
- Your home telephone number including area code
- Your parents' cell phone numbers

This information will help you if you are ever lost.